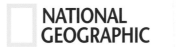

Which One Is Different?

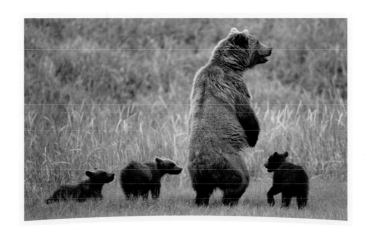

Doug Oxenford

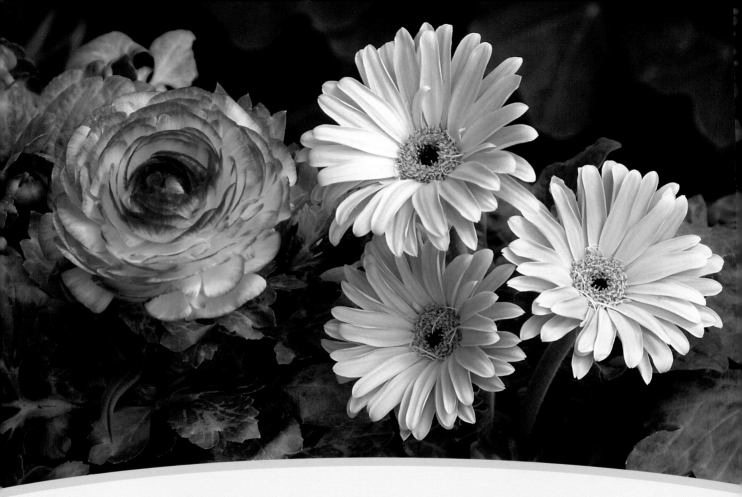

Which flower is different?

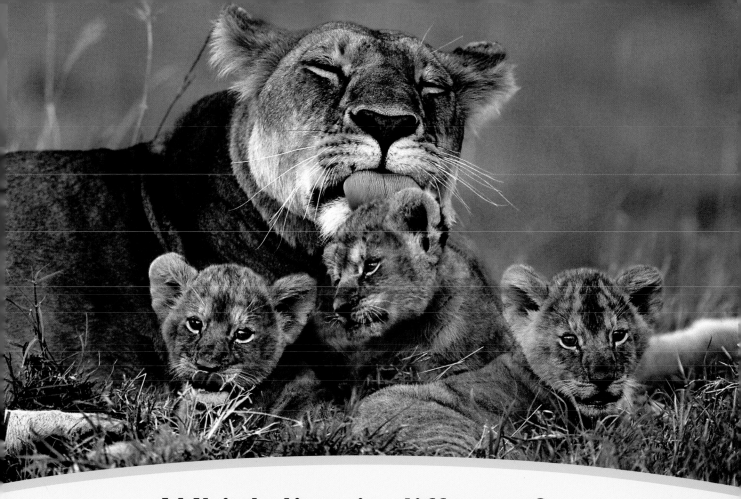

Which lion is different?

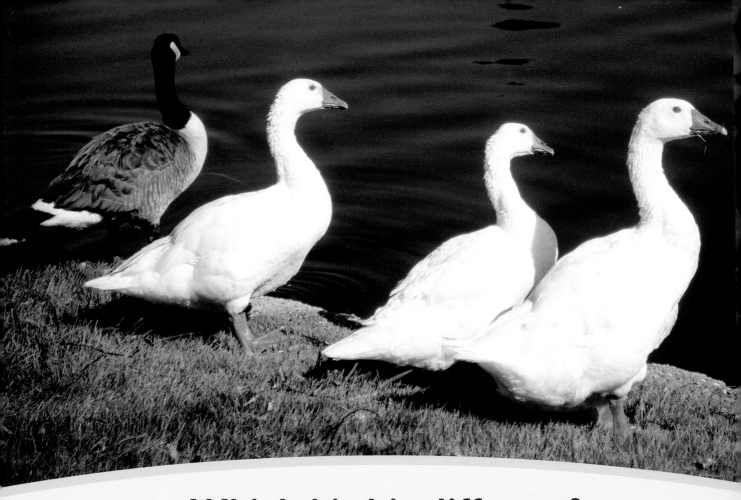

Which bird is different?

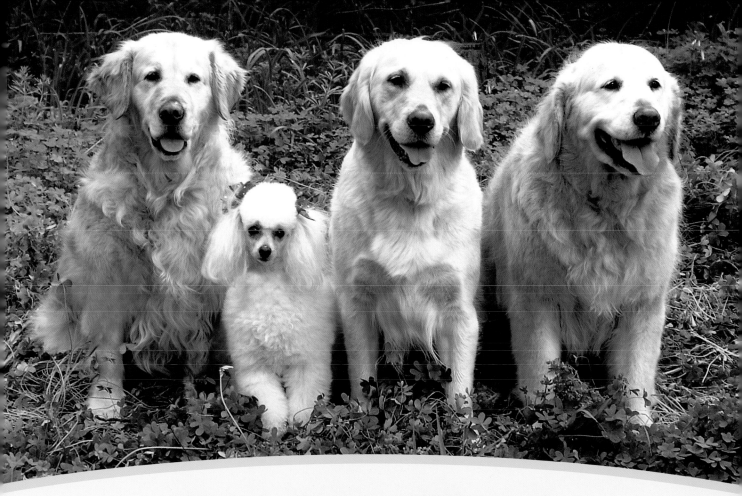

Which dog is different?

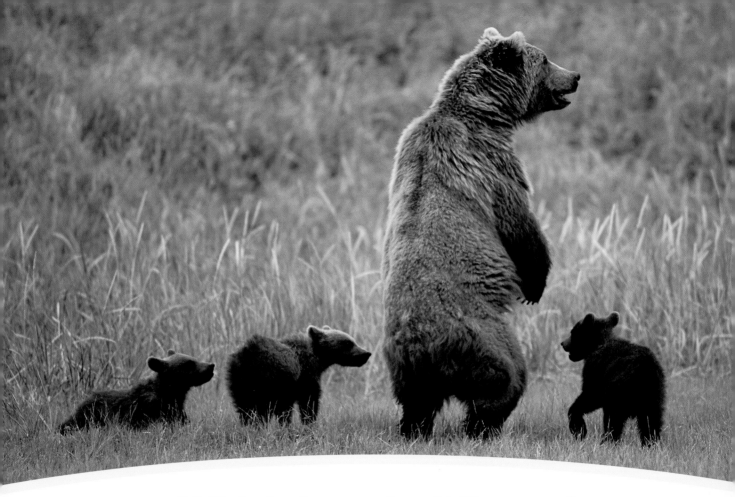

Which bear is different?

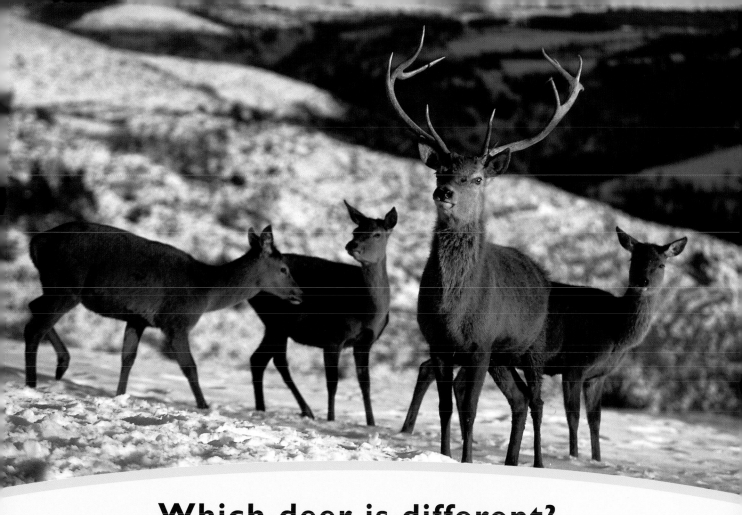

Which deer is different?

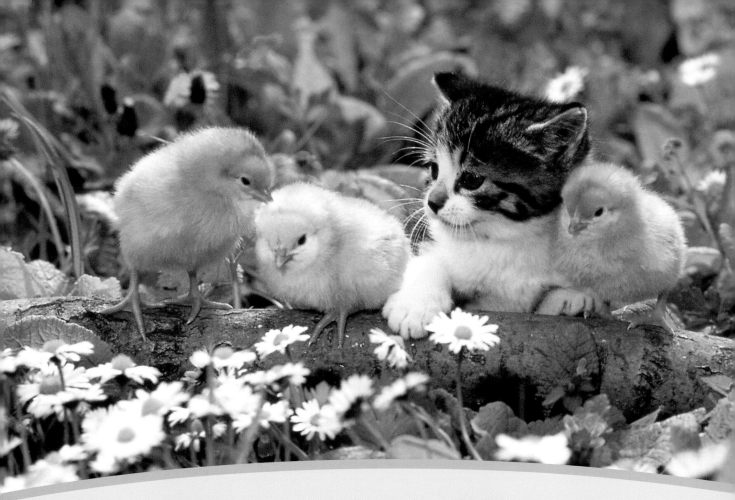

Which animal is different?